CALMING
COLOURING
FOR
kids

Buster Books

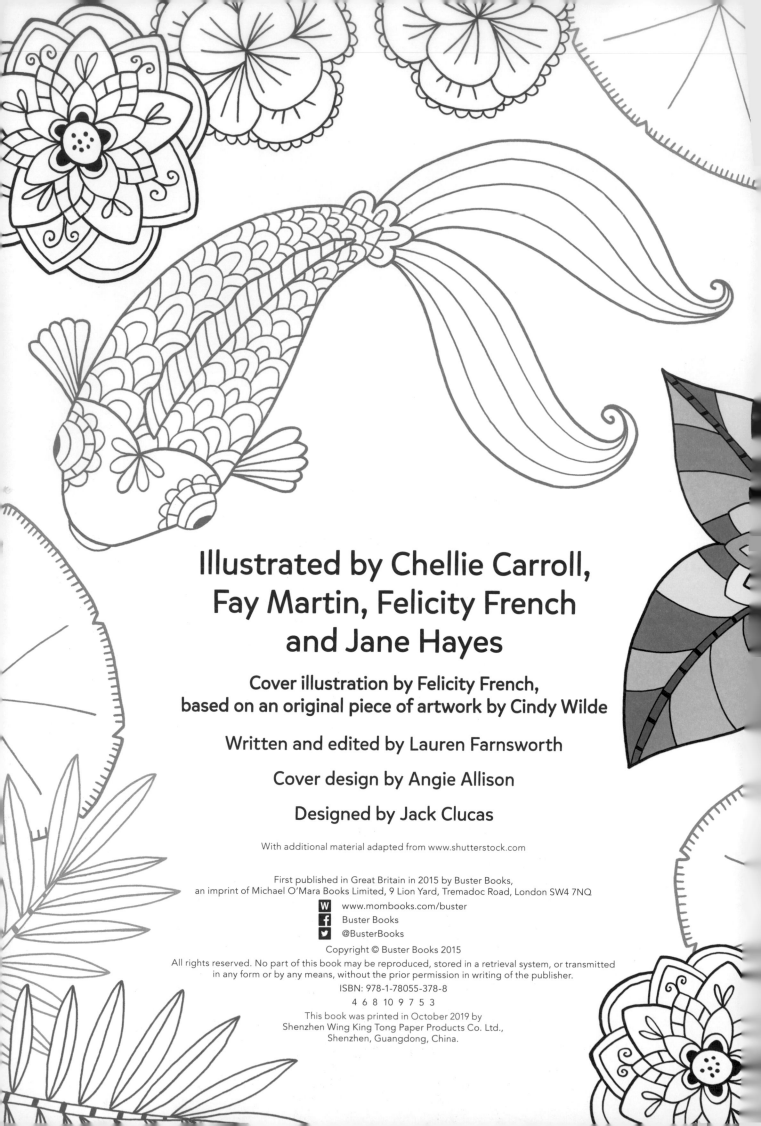

Illustrated by Chellie Carroll,
Fay Martin, Felicity French
and Jane Hayes

Cover illustration by Felicity French,
based on an original piece of artwork by Cindy Wilde

Written and edited by Lauren Farnsworth

Cover design by Angie Allison

Designed by Jack Clucas

With additional material adapted from www.shutterstock.com

First published in Great Britain in 2015 by Buster Books,
an imprint of Michael O'Mara Books Limited, 9 Lion Yard, Tremadoc Road, London SW4 7NQ

www.mombooks.com/buster
Buster Books
@BusterBooks

ISBN: 978-1-78055-378-8

4 6 8 10 9 7 5 3

This book was printed in October 2019 by
Shenzhen Wing King Tong Paper Products Co. Ltd.,
Shenzhen, Guangdong, China.

Sometimes concentrating on doing something creative can help take your mind off things you are worrying about. In this book there's a mixture of beautiful colouring pages for you to complete and doodling pages to cover with your own patterns and designs. Use any shades you like and don't worry about staying inside the lines!

Each colour has a group of pictures. You might find that different colours make you feel different things. Blues and greens, for example, might make you feel tranquil – like you are drifting on an ocean – but reds and oranges might make you feel strong and energetic.

Enjoy filling in this book.

RED

Red is courageous.
An energetic, bold colour,
it might make you feel
strong and fiery.

ORANGE

Orange is excitable. Warm and glowing, it might make you feel eager and determined.

YELLOW

Yellow is happy. The colour of sunshine, it can make you feel like smiling and laughing.

GREEN

Green is peaceful, calm and
pure. Like walking through
a forest, it can make you
feel refreshed.

BLUE

Blue is calm. It is sleepy and quiet. This colour can make you feel relaxed, like listening to the waves of the ocean.

PURPLE

Purple is quiet. Dusky
and gentle, it might
make you feel lazy
like a cloudy sky.

PINK

Pink is shy. Delicate and blushing, it can make you feel quiet and soft.

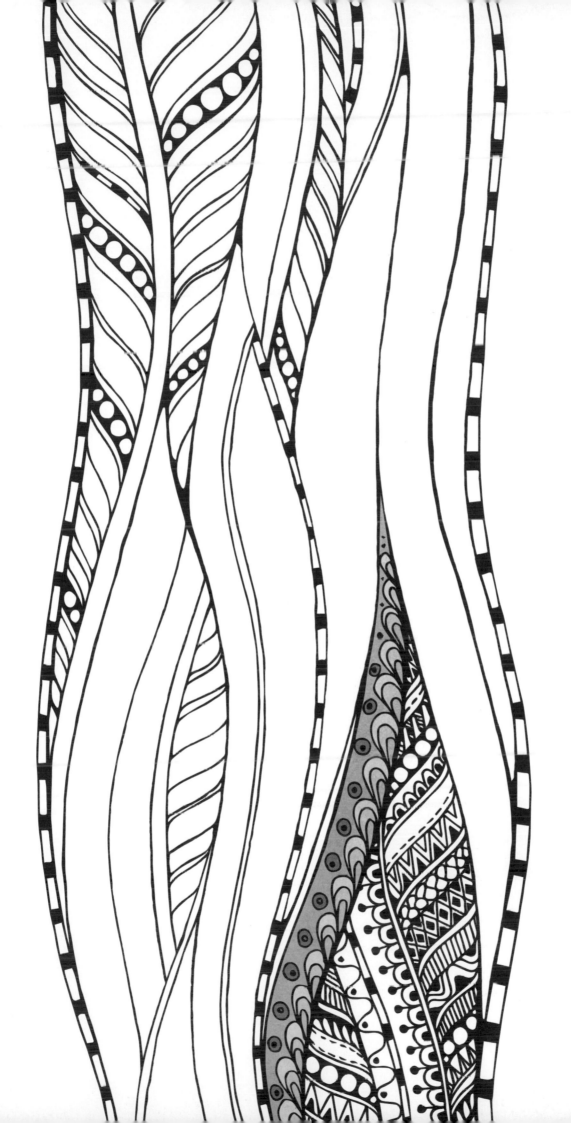

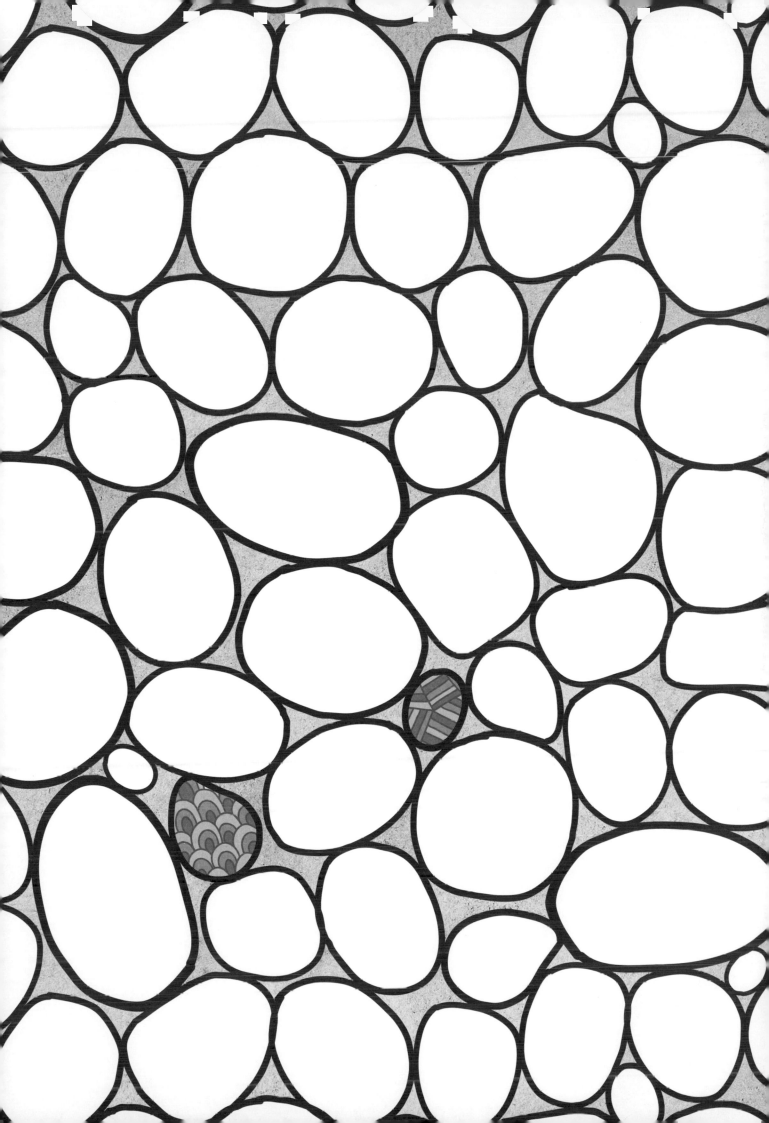

BLACK

Black is the colour of the night. It is dark and secret, but can also be filled with colour and light.